POSTERS!

It's time for a *Rebirth*! In this issue, Batman enters a new beginning, with a new partner, and an old enemy! Plus, *Robin: Son of Batman* reaches its stunning conclusion, and in *Batman Eternal*, Alfred teams up with a highly unlikely ally! If you have anything to say about the issue, let us know at batmancomicuk@titanemail.com!

BATMAN

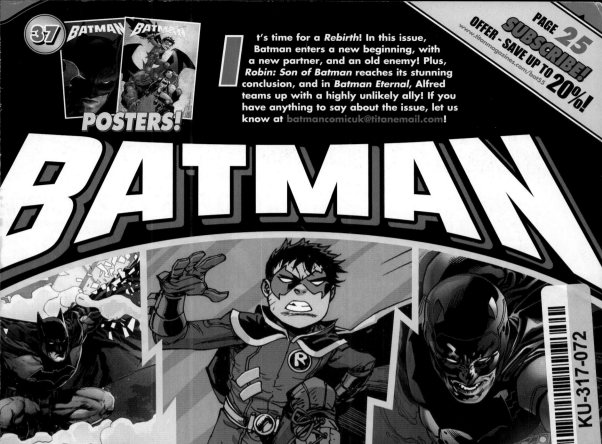

KU-317-072

5

First printed in *Batman: Rebirth #1*

BATMAN - 'BATMAN: REBIRTH'

It's a new era for Batman, as we see a year in the life of the Dark Knight! Duke Thomas comes looking for a job, and he and Batman soon come to blows with the Calendar Man, time and time again...

Writers: Scott Snyder and Tom King • **Artist:** Mikel Janin • **Colourist:** June Chung • **Letterer:** Deron Bennett

27

ROBIN, SON OF BATMAN - 'IT NEVER ENDS'

It's the finale to Damian Wayne's quest for atonement! In the wake of their last victory, Damian, Maya and Goliath find that there's still one enemy left to beat, and it could be the most terrible one of all! Can all of them survive the encounter?

First printed in *Robin, Son of Batman #13*

Writer: Ray Fawkes • **Artist:** Ramon Bachs • **Colorist:** Mat Lopes • **Letterer:** Deron Bennett

54

BATMAN ETERNAL - 'BURIED DEEP'

Arkham is just a crater in the ground, and the inmates are escaping, as the police try to contain them! Meanwhile, Julia does her best to fill in for her father, who has his own problems, as he is forced into teaming up with... Bane?!

First printed in *Batman Eternal #31*

Story: Scott Snyder and James Tynion IV • **Script:** Ray Fawkes • **Consulting Writers:** Kyle Higgins and Tim Seeley • **Penciller:** Fernando Pasarin • **Inker:** Matt Ryan • **Colourist:** Blond • **Letterer:** Taylor Esposito

EDITORIAL
Editor Neil Edwards
Designer Donna Askem
Editorial Assistants Tolly Maggs, Lauren McPhee
Senior Comics Editor Martin Eden

TITAN MAGAZINES
Production Manager Obi Onuora
Production Supervisors Maria Pearson,

Jackie Flook
Production Assistant Peter James
Art Director Oz Browne
Senior Sales Manager Steve Tothill
Direct Sales and Marketing Manager Ricky Claydon
Brand Manager, Marketing Lucy Ripper
Commercial Manager Michelle Fairlamb
Marketing and Advertising Assistant Jessica Reid

Publishing Manager Darryl Tothill
Publishing Director Chris Teather
Operations Director Leigh Baulch
Executive Director Vivian Cheung
Publisher Nick Landau

DISTRIBUTION
UK Newsstand: Comag
Tel: 01895 433600
Account Manager: Peter Hilton

UK Direct Sales Market:
Diamond Comic Distributors
Subscriptions:
Tel: 0844 322 1246

www.titanmagazines.com/batman

ADVERTISING HOTLINE:
Tel: 020 7620 0200

SHE'S LEWD AND CRUDE
AND KICKING BUTT WITH POWER GIRL

3 AWESOME STORIES!

HARLEY QUINN IS DRIVEN MAD BY HER POWER RING AND TAKES ON GREEN LANTERN!

HARLEY QUINN AND POWER GIRL TAKE ON THE SPORTSMASTER AND THE CLOCK KING!

IS POWER GIRL AND HARLEY QUINN'S PARTNERSHIP ABOUT TO REACH AN END?

#3 ON SALE NOW!

HARLEY QUINN - NOW IN HER OWN COMIC!

HARLEY QUINN #3

FREE POSTERS!

SPACE GIRLS!

HARLEY GETS A POWER RING!

MONDAY: SPRING.

:ANNNGHH:

MISTER WAYNE, WHEN IT'S 137 DEGREES IN GOTHAM WITHOUT A HINT OF A BREEZE...

...TRADITION USUALLY HOLDS THAT ONE SCHEDULES MEETINGS INSIDE.

YEAH, WELL, YOU KNOW ME, LUCIUS...

THAT'S INSANE.

HE LOOKS *OLDER*.

HE IS. *JULIAN DAY'S* BODY AGES WITH THE SEASONS.

A TRUE *"CALENDAR MAN,"* HE DIES IN WINTER, MOLTS HIS SKIN, AND IS *REBORN* A YOUNG MAN IN HIS PRIME.

MOLTS? YIKES. SO HIS AGING, IT MEANS--

IT MEANS HE'S *SPEEDING UP* THE SEASONS BY SOME HIDDEN MECHANISM. TOMORROW THE TEMPERATURE WILL DROP. THEN RISE...

HE MUST HAVE HIDDEN SPORES AROUND THE CITY. THEY'LL *HATCH* ON THURSDAY WITH THE COMING OF SPRING. HE'LL NEVER TALK, EITHER.

WE NEED TO GO.

BRUCE, WAIT. I NEED TO ASK...

"GOOD, MISTER THOMAS.

"THEN I NEED YOU TO *COUNT.*

"OXYGEN TANK'S USELESS IN WATER THIS TEMPERATURE. FREEZES THE MAIN VALVE.

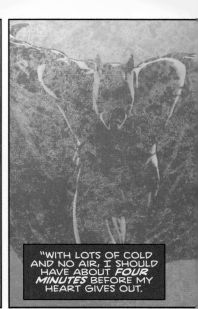

"WITH LOTS OF COLD AND NO AIR, I SHOULD HAVE ABOUT *FOUR MINUTES* BEFORE MY HEART GIVES OUT.

"IF I CAN'T FIND AND DISABLE CALENDAR'S MACHINE IN THOSE FOUR MINUTES, THE MACHINE'LL TURN THE CITY TO SPRING AGAIN.

"ALL THOSE *SPORES* WILL ACTIVATE. AND *GOTHAM* DIES.

"SO I NEED YOU TO *COUNT.*"

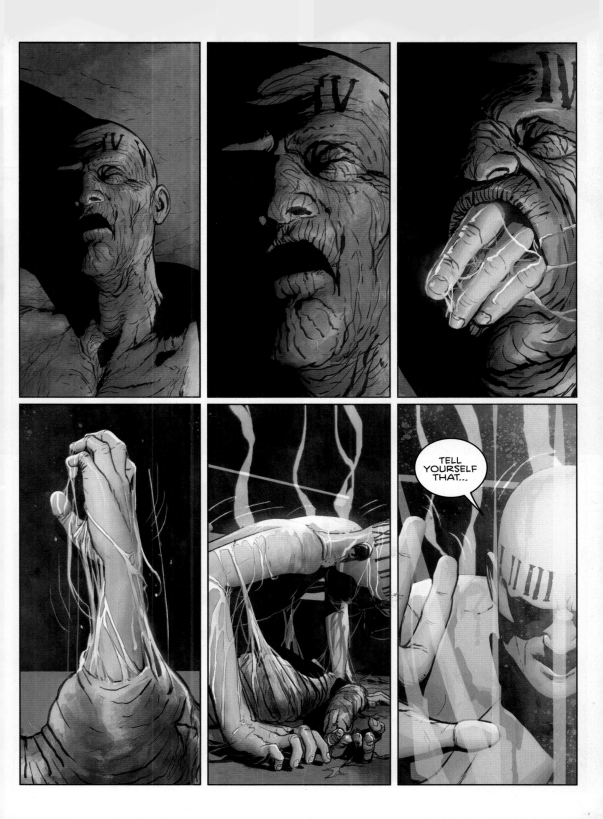

"...TELL YOURSELF IT'S DONE.

"BUT IT'S NEVER *DONE.*"

AGAIN.

HE'S BACK. RIGHT ABOUT NOW, HE'S... *HATCHING.* I WAS LOOKING AT THE FILE ON HIM.

IT SAYS THAT EVERY TIME HE COMES BACK, HE COMES BACK SLIGHTLY DIFFERENT, HIS DNA ALTERED. HE'S A DIFFERENT PERSON, BUT HE RETAINS ALL THE MEMORIES HE HAD LAST TIME.

HE'LL COME UP WITH NEW IDEAS.

THE TREE IS WINNING. YOUR POINT?

JUST THAT, HE COMES BACK *BETTER* EVERY TIME. HOW ARE WE SUPPOSED TO COMBAT THAT?

EASY. *WE* COME BACK BETTER EACH TIME, TOO.

...

YOU'RE CRAZY, YOU KNOW THAT, RIGHT?

NEXT ISSUE: GOTHAM'S NEW HERO

SUBSCRIBE
TO BATMAN REBIRTH

BATMAN REBIRTH STARTS HERE!

REBIRTH #1

BATMAN

HAS ROBIN MET HIS MATCH?

YEAR OF THE BATMAN

SAVE UP TO **15%**

WHY SUBSCRIBE?

- **PAY JUST £20.50* EVERY 12 MONTHS!**
- **6 ISSUES FOR THE PRICE OF 5!**
- **FREE UK DELIVERY TO YOUR DOOR!**
- **NEVER MISS AN ISSUE!**

VISIT:
TITANMAGAZINES.COM/REBIRTH1
OR CALL 0844 322 1246

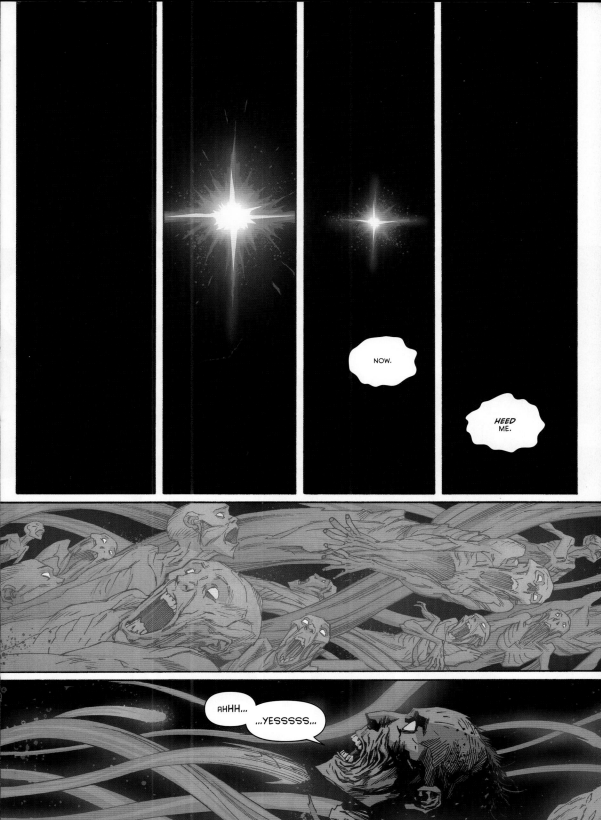

REEEEUUNK!

THE LU'UN DARGA HAVE FOUND US AGAIN!

WHAT ARE THERE, LIKE, TEN MILLION OF THESE GUYS?

YOUR DAD MUST'VE OFFERED SOME KINDA SWEET NINJA SIGNING BONUS, SUREN, OR—

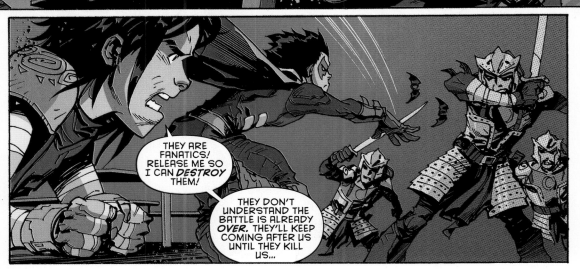

THEY ARE FANATICS! RELEASE ME SO I CAN DESTROY THEM!

THEY DON'T UNDERSTAND THE BATTLE IS ALREADY OVER. THEY'LL KEEP COMING AFTER US UNTIL THEY KILL US...

...Meeeee.

ROBIN! THERE'S SOME KINDA *ENERGY* DRAIN...

SLAP

HERE. FREQUENCY DISRUPTER! THAT'LL KEEP HIM WITH US FOR NOW. CAN YOU CALL FOR HELP? YOUR DAD OR SOMEONE?

MY COMMS ARE OFFLINE.

THIS IS *DARGA* SPIRIT MAGIC!

ONE OF SUREN'S FAMILY IS STILL *ACTIVE* SOMEWHERE. HE WAS WRONG. THIS BATTLE ISN'T OVER YET.

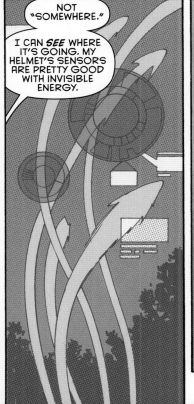

NOT "SOMEWHERE."

I CAN *SEE* WHERE IT'S GOING. MY HELMET'S SENSORS ARE PRETTY GOOD WITH INVISIBLE ENERGY.

THEN LET'S GO...

THEY'RE ALL BEING DRAINED! WHATEVER THIS IS, IT SEEMS TO TARGET ONLY THE LU'UN DARGA!

BUT BE *CAREFUL!* WE DON'T KNOW WHAT THEIR ENERGY IS *FEEDING!*

WE OUGHT TO— →*Hoough!*←

BLANGGG

→*Agh!*←

GOLIATH...

...TAKE ME THERE...

→*Tt*←

I THOUGHT YOUR HELMET WAS GOOD WITH *INVISIBLE ENERGY.*

NOBODY'S *PERFECT.*

I THOUGHT YOU'RE SUPPOSED TO *BE* NOBODY.

OH, HA, HA.

WAIT, GOLIATH! DON'T--

THERE! I SEE SOMEONE!

ARE YOU READY?

ON THREE. ONE...

...TWO...

...THREE!

POW

BOOM

BOOM

BOOM

NO. TOO *EASY.* IT'S--

AH HA HA HA HA!

BATMAN™

YOU YET LIVE!

YES...

SUREN! DON'T LET HIM *TOUCH* YOU!

THUNK

THUNK

THUNK

→Hrrrgh!←

THIS SPIRIT BATTERY IS MY *CONTINGENCY*. PREPARED MILLENNIA AGO, TO BE REALIZED ONLY IF THE PROPER LU'UN DARGA APOCALYPSE WAS *THWARTED*.

THAT IT HAS ACTIVATED WHILE YOU ARE STILL *ALIVE* DEMONSTRATES YOUR *FAILURE*. YOUR *WEAKNESS*...

...THAT YOU WOULD LET YOURSELF *LIVE* AFTER FAILING ME DEMONSTRATES YOUR *COWARDICE* AND *INCOMPETENCE*.

FILTH. DID YOU LEARN *NOTHING* AT MY SIDE?

FATHER... YOU *LIED* TO US.

OUR SOULS WILL NOT LIVE ON IN THE NEW WORLD, WILL THEY?

THEY JUST EMPOWER YOUR MAGIC. *YOU* WILL REMAIN.

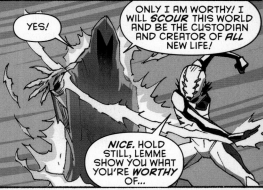

YES!

ONLY I AM WORTHY! I WILL *SCOUR* THIS WORLD AND BE THE CUSTODIAN AND CREATOR OF *ALL* NEW LIFE!

NICE. HOLD STILL, LEMME SHOW YOU WHAT YOU'RE *WORTHY* OF...

YOU WERE MERELY A WEAPON TO BRING IT ABOUT WHILE I *SLEPT*.

AND NOW TO *FINISH* THIS...

HE'S RIGHT. THE POWER GOING INTO THAT THING, IT'S *INSANE!*

IT'S NOT SLOWING DOWN AT ALL!

HEH... HAH...

MY BODY CAN *FAIL.* THIS SPELL WILL COMPLETE ITSELF REGARDLESS.

THE TRUE VICTORY OF DEN DARGA IS AT *HAND.* ALL YOUR *HOPES,* ALL YOUR *STRUGGLE...*

...IT WILL ALL MEAN *NOTHING.*

WHAT DO WE *DO?*

ROBIN? WHAT DO WE DO?

→*Tt*←

HE *TOLD* US.

IT'S A *BATTERY.*

SUREN. DID YOU LEARN TO *PULL* SPIRITS LIKE YOUR FATHER CAN? *STEER* THEM?

A... LITTLE...

CRACK

GOOD.

WHAK

DO IT NOW! GUIDE THEM ALONG THESE *WIRES!*

WE CAN SHORT IT OUT!

THE DISCHARGE... WILL *KILL* YOU, AL GHUL.

AND I WILL *REMAIN* TO DESTROY YOUR FRIENDS AND BUILD MY SPELL ANEW. EVEN IF IT TAKES *CENTURIES*...

I ENDURED THE *YEAR OF BLOOD* AND TAUGHT THE *AL GHULS* THAT I AM WORTHY TO *RULE* THIS WORLD, DEN DARGA.

AND THEN THROUGH THE *YEAR OF ATONEMENT,* I TAUGHT MYSELF THAT I AM WORTHY TO *FREE* IT FROM THE LIKES OF YOU *AND* THE AL GHULS.

NO!

THERE'S *GOT* TO BE ANOTHER WAY!

GOLIATH! ANYONE WHO TOUCHES ME... WILL CARRY THE SHOCK, TOO... STOP MAYA...

GO!

REEEEEUUNKK!

~Hnnf!~

KKKKKTTTTKKT...

HE...HE *DID* IT...

DO YOU FEEL IT? IT'S STOPPED.

YEAH, BUT...

...HE'S *DEAD*.

REEE?

NO. NO, DAMIAN, NO...

IT'S NOT FAIR, IT'S NOT *RIGHT*...

YOU SAVED THE *WORLD*. MORE THAN *ONCE*.

BUT YOU DON'T--

WAIT. WHAT'S THAT?

HIS SPIRIT! I CAN *SEE* IT! IT'S NOT FAR!

IT'S RIGHT *HERE!*

CAN HE HEAR ME? IF I TALK TO HIM?

DAMIAN? CAN YOU HEAR ME?

DAMIAN! SON OF AL GHUL!

DON'T...

...DON'T CALL HIM THAT...

THAT'S NOT WHO HE IS...

WE STILL HAVE TO DO ALL KINDS OF STUFF...

...WE STILL HAVE TO FINISH THAT ICE CREAM.

~TT~

IT WASN'T *THAT* GOOD.

DAMIAN!

WELL...IT LOOKS LIKE WE SUCCEEDED. DEN DARGA IS FINISHED.

WELL DONE, EVERYONE.

OH FOR--

HEY, MAYBE YOU COULD SAY *THANK YOU* OR SOMETHING? WE ONLY JUST PULLED YOU BACK FROM LITERAL *DEATH* WITH OUR SINCERE HEARTS OR WHATEVER...

...NO BIG *DEAL.*

YES. AS I SAID.

WELL DONE.

-kktt- ROBIN. ROBIN, COME IN.

YES, BATMAN, I CAN HEAR YOU. MY COMMS ARE BACK.

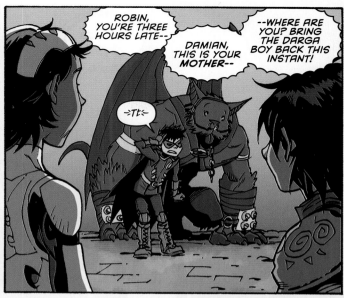
ROBIN, YOU'RE THREE HOURS LATE--

DAMIAN, THIS IS YOUR MOTHER--

--WHERE ARE YOU? BRING THE DARGA BOY BACK THIS INSTANT!

-Tt-

--IS EVERYTHING ALL RIGHT? I CAN PICK YOU UP IF YOU NEED A RIDE.

DAMIAN, I THOUGHT WE HAD AN UNDERSTANDING. YOU--

THANK YOU, TALIA. THANK YOU, FATHER. I'M FINE!

KLIK

WELL?

WHAT ARE YOU ALL WAITING FOR?

ADVENTURE AWAITS...

THE HOME OF SUPERHEROES!

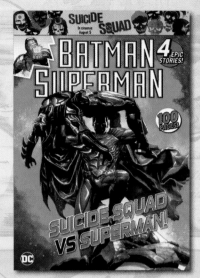

REBIRTH

You'll no doubt have noticed the word 'Rebirth' on the front cover of this very magazine you're reading right now. But what is Rebirth? Rebirth is an exciting new era for Titan Comics' super hero titles, and you've got a privileged sneak peek at it in this magazine, with our launch of *Batman: Rebirth*, which marks the start of something very different for the Dark Knight himself. Batman has a new partner, a new version of his classic costume and soon to come, some friends and foes both old and new, with new looks of their own!

And it doesn't end there! Soon we'll be rolling out Rebirth content across our whole stable of magazines, with new looks, stories and directions for all your favorite characters, from The Flash to Green Arrow, Wonder Woman to Harley Quinn!

In the words of DC Comics' Chief Creative Officer Geoff Johns, "Some things alter and change, but it's more character-driven, and it's also more about revealing secrets and mysteries within the DC Universe."

Many characters not seen in a long time will return, and there are more exciting changes to come with our magazines, includin[g] new series of *Harley Quinn* and *Suicide Squad*. We're not exaggerating when we say that thi[s] will be one of the most tremendous eras in ou[r] super hero comics yet!

Look out for Rebirth coming to our range of super hero magazines soon!

ARKHAM ASYLUM DISASTER SITE.

SCOTT SNYDER & JAMES TYNION IV story   RAY FAWKES script
KYLE HIGGINS & TIM SEELEY consulting writers   FERNANDO PASARIN pencils
MATT RYAN inks BLOND colors TAYLOR ESPOSITO letters   RAFAEL ALBUQUERQUE cover
DAVE WIELGOSZ asst. editor   CHRIS CONROY editor   MARK DOYLE group editor
BATMAN CREATED BY BOB KANE

THEY'RE COVERING ALL THE ANGLES UP THERE. THERE'S NO CHANCE YOU CAN MAKE IT BACK OUT THAT WAY.

I'M MAPPING OUT AN ESCAPE ROUTE THROUGH THE TUNNELS *NOW.*

BATMAN, CAN YOU *READ* ME?

OH. OH *NO.*

I *GOT* ONE HERE!

HEY, GIVE ME A *HAND!*

HERE, TAKE *MINE.*

KKKTTT

"THIS ISN'T *RIGHT*..."

...IT'S SUPPOSED TO--YOU KNOW-- EXPLODE AND STUFF.

BITS OF BATS. EHEHEH.

TIK TIK TIK

HEY!

WHOK

CRACK

THIS IS PLASTICINE.

SOMEBODY'S PLAYING GAMES.

BATMAN... UP ON THE SURFACE.

IT'S MISTER FREEZE...

BLAM BLAM

LIEUTENANT BULLOCK. *BATMAN.*

ARE WE *CLEAR?*

NO. NO CLEARANCE ON THE BAT.

NOT FROM *ME.*

BUT *SIR!*

ZSASZ IS DOWN.

MISTER FREEZE SHOULD BE IN *PLAIN VIEW.*

I HAVE HIM.

YOU *DO,* DON'T YOU?

INFRARED IS SHOWING *THE IMPERCEPTIBLE MAN* MOVING TO THE WEST. LOOKS LIKE HE'S INVISIBLE IN THE NORMAL SPECTRUM.

I'M PATCHING THE FEED INTO YOUR LENSES.

OKAY. SORRY.

I HAVE THE SATELLITES RUNNING THE SEARCH FOR HUSH.

NOW WE JUST NEED TO HOPE HE STEPS INTO OUR VIEW SOMEWHERE.

GOOD WORK, PENNY-TWO...

THIS IS ALL WRONG.

UNSCRAMBLING THE HOSPITAL RECORDS NOW.

EITHER THEY HAD SOME KIND OF COMPREHENSIVE SYSTEM MALFUNCTION...

...OR THEY'VE BEEN HIT WITH A VIRUS DESIGNED TO *LOOK* LIKE ONE.

BLOODY HELL, I'M STARTING TO THINK LIKE *YOU*.

GOOD. THE SOONER THE BETTER.

IT'S NOT *PARANOIA* IF EVERYONE'S REALLY OUT TO--

OH, GOD.

THIS BETTER BE A *LIE*.

PATIENT: PENNYWORTH, ALFRED

TRANSFERRED TO CUSTODY ARKHAM MAXIMUM SECURITY PER STATE SUBPOENA ORDER #4420551

MY FATHER...

HE'S *IN* ARKHAM.

HE'S BEEN THERE SINCE *YESTERDAY!*

DOWNTOWN GOTHAM.

SCREEECH!

POW

CRAK

OH CRAP--

VROOOOM

WHUDD

OKAY. *THERE* YOU ARE. HAD TO HANDLE THIS *MYSELF,* DIDN'T I?

Gguh!

ALL GOOD THINGS, *huh?*

IT'S ABOUT *TIME.*

ggod

NEXT: WEAPONS OF MASS DESTRUCTION